clapton chr

the best of eric clapton

ISBN 0-634-01661-X

HAL•LEONARD®
CORPORATION
7777 W. BLUEMOUND RD. P.O. BOX 13819 MILWAUKEE, WI 53213

Visit Hal Leonard Online at
www.halleonard.com

blue eyes blue

words & music by diane warren

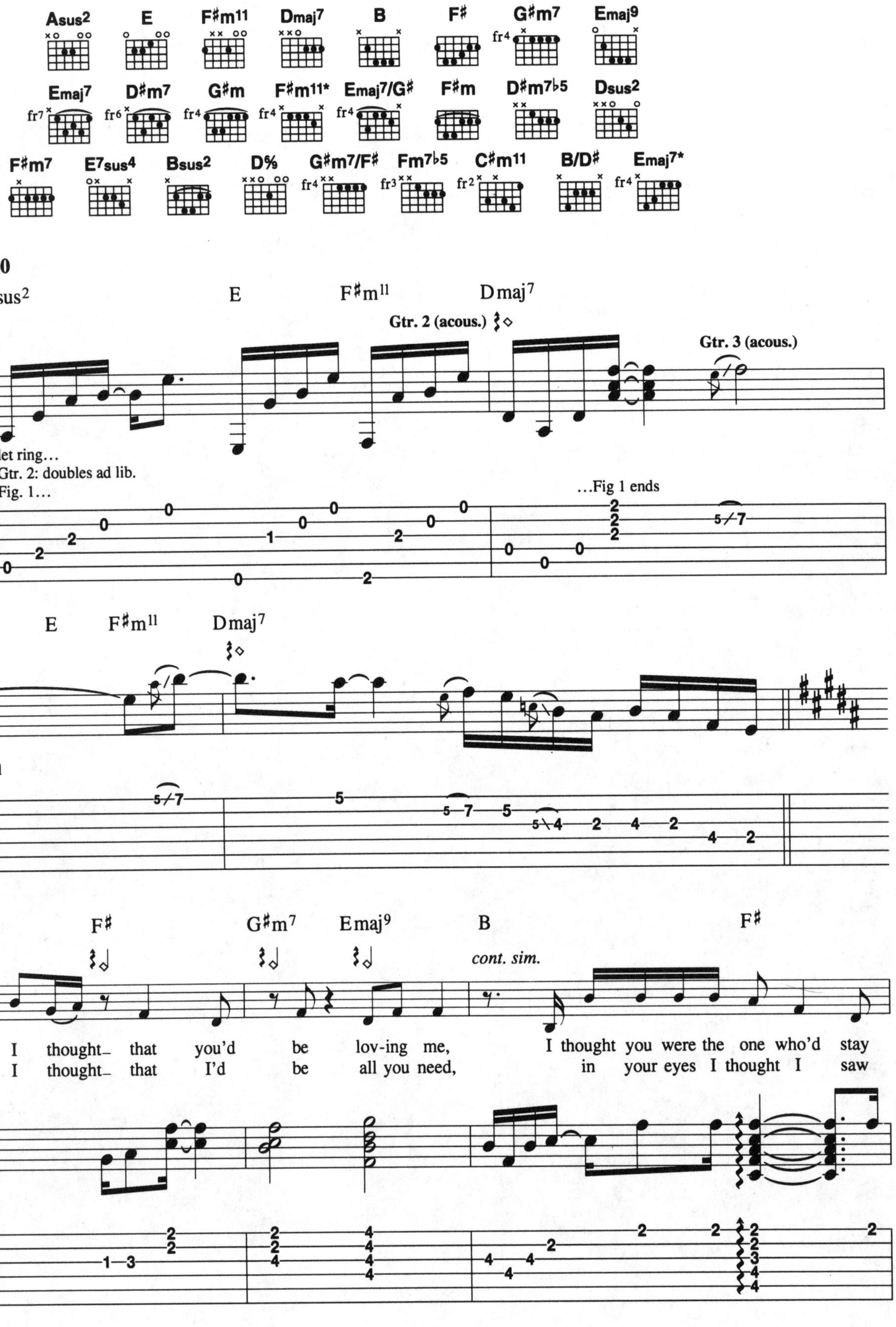

G♯m7 Emaj9 B F♯ G♯m7 Emaj9
for - ev - er. But now for - ev - er's come and gone, and I'm
my hea - ven. And now my hea - ven's gone a - way, and I'm
B F♯ G♯m7 Emaj9
still here a - lone. 'Cause you were on - ly
out in the cold. 'Cause you had me be -
Pre-chorus
Gtr. 2 (acous.)
Emaj7 D♯m7 G♯m F♯
play - ing, you were on - ly play - ing with my heart. I was nev - er
- liev - ing, you had me be - liev - ing in a lie. Guess I could-n't
Emaj7 D♯m7 F♯m11* Emaj7/G♯
wait - ing, I was nev - er wait - ing for the tears to start.
see it, I guess I could-n't see it 'til I saw good-bye.
B
½

Chorus
Asus2 E F♯m11 Dmaj7
It was you who put the clouds a-round me,
Gtr. 1 (acous.)
Asus2 E F♯m11 Dmaj7
it was you who made the tears fall down.
Gtr. 3 (acous.)
F♯m (E bass) D♯m7(♭5) Dsus2
It was you who broke my heart in pie-ces. It was you, it was you,
Gtr. 4 (acous.)
1.
F♯m7 E7sus4 Asus2 E F♯m11 Dmaj7
who made my blue eyes blue. Oh, I nev-er should have trust-ed you.
B
Gtr. 1: w/Fig. 1
Full
T
A
B

2.
Dmaj7 E7sus4 Asus2 E F#m11 Dmaj7
who made my blue eyes blue. Oh, I nev-er should have trust-ed you.
Full
Gtr. 1: w/Fig. 1
Solo
Bsus2 F# G#m7 Emaj9
Full
Bsus2 F# G#m7 Emaj9
1½
Full
Bsus2 F# G#m7 Emaj9

Bsus2 F# G#m Emaj9
'Cause you were on - ly
8va
B
Full
Pre-chorus Emaj7 D#m7 F#m11 Emaj7/G#
play - ing, you were on - ly play - ing with— my heart. I was nev - er
Gtr. 2 (acous.)
Emaj7 D#m7 F#m11 Emaj7/G#
wait - ing,—— I was nev - er wait - ing for— the tears— to start.
Gtr. 3 (acous.)
Chorus Asus2 E F#m11 D6/9 Asus2 E
It was you— who put the clouds a - round me. It was you.—
Gtr. 1 (acous.)
Strings arr. for Gtr.

Bsus2 F♯ G♯m7 Emaj9
It was you, who put those clouds a-round me.
Full
Bsus2 F♯ G♯m7 Emaj9
It was you, who made the tears fall down.
Gtr. 1 (acous.)
Gtr. 3 (acous.)
Full
G♯m7 /F♯ Fm7(♭5)
On - ly you, who broke my heart in pie - ces.
8va
Full
Gtr. 1 (acous.)
loco
C♯m11 B/D♯ Emaj7* F♯m11*
It was you, it was you, who made my blue eyes blue.

Bsus2 F♯ G♯m7 Emaj9
Oh, I nev - er should have trust - ed you.
Gtr. 3 (acous.)
Pre
Full
Bsus2 F♯ G♯m7 Emaj9
Oh, nev - er should have trust - ed you.
(B)
8va
Bsus2 F♯ G♯m7 Emaj9
Oh, I nev - er should have trust - ed you.
(8va)
loco
rall.
Bsus2 F♯ G♯m7 Emaj9
Oh, I nev - er should have trust - ed you.

change the world

words & music by tommy sims, gordon kennedy & wayne kirkpatrick

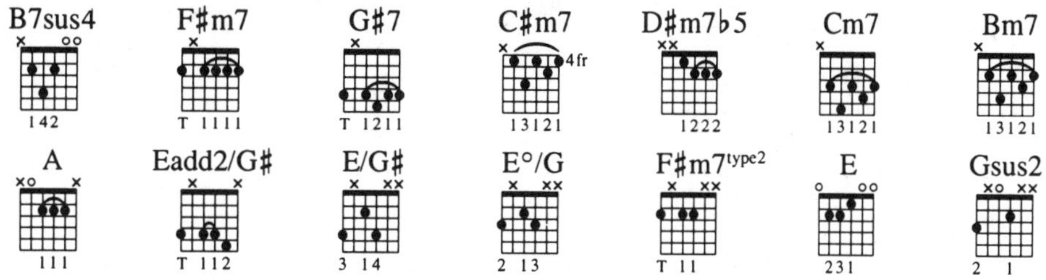

Verse
Gtr. 3 tacet
E A/E E7(no3rd) A/E E
1. If I could reach the stars, pull one down for you.
Rhy. Fig. 2
A/E E7(no3rd) A/E E
Shine it on my heart so you could see the truth.
A D/A A7(no3rd)
Then this love I have in - side

D/A
A
E
A/E
E7(no3rd)
is ev - 'ry - thing it ___ seems. ___
But ___ for now I find ___
1/2
1/4
it's on - ly in my ___ dreams. ___
And I can
G#7
End Rhy. Fig. 2
(cont. in slash)
Chorus
Gtr. 2 tacet
F#m7
Rhy. Fig. 3
Gtr. 1
C#m7
D#m7b5
change ___ the world. ___
(Change ___ the world. ___
I will be ___ the sun - light ___ in your
I will be ___ the sun - light in your
u - ni - verse. ___
u - ni - verse.
You would think ___ my love ___ was real - ly
You would think ___ my love, ___
Gtr. 2

C♯m7 Cm7 Bm7 A Eadd2/G♯
End Rhy. Fig. 3
some - thing good, ba - by, if I could
some - thing good.)
E/G♯ E°/G F♯m7type2
Gtr. 1
change the world.
Gtr. 2
Gtr. 3
Rhy. Fill 1
End Rhy. Fill 1
*vol. knob swell
Interlude
Gtr. 1: w/ Rhy Fig. 1, simile
Gtr. 3 tacet
E F♯m7 Gadd2 F♯m7 E
Verse
Gtr. 1: w/ Rhy. Fig. 2, simile
E A/E E7(no3rd) A/E E
2. If I could be king, e - ven for a day,

A/E E7(no3rd) A/E E
I'd take you as my queen, I'd have it no oth - er way.
1/2 1/4
A D/A A7(no3rd) D/A A
And our love would rule in this king - dom we have made.
1/4
E A/E E7(no3rd)
Till then I'd be a fool,
A/E G#7
wish - ing for the day. And I can
Chorus
Gtr. 1: w/ Rhy. Fig. 3
Gtr. 2 tacet, 1st time; w/ Fill 1, 2nd time
F#m7 G#7 C#m7
change the world.
(Change the, change the world.
Fill 1
Gtr. 2
T
A
B

Gtr. 2: Fill 2, 2nd time
D#m7♭5 G#7 C#m7
I will be the sun - light in your u - ni - verse.
I will be the sun - light in your u - ni - verse.
To Coda
D#m7♭5 G#7 C#m7 Cm7 Bm7
You would think my love was real - ly some - thing good, ba - by,
You would think my love, some - thing good, oh,
A Eadd2/G# E/G# E°/G F#m7 E
Gtr. 3
if I could change the world, ba - by,
if I could, yeah.)
Gtr. 2
Gtr. 1
Fill 2
Gtr. 2

Gtr. 2 & 3 tacet
A7
Eadd2/G#
Gtr. 3: w/ Rhy. Fill 1
E/G#
E°/G
F#m7
if I could change the world.
Gtr. 1
Guitar Solo
Gtr. 1: w/ Rhy. Fig. 1 1½ times, simile
E
F#m7
Gadd2
F#m7
E
Gtr. 2
1/2
full
1/4
F#m7
Gadd2
full
D.S. al Coda
F#m7
G#7
I can
Gtr. 2
1/2
1/4
Gtr. 1

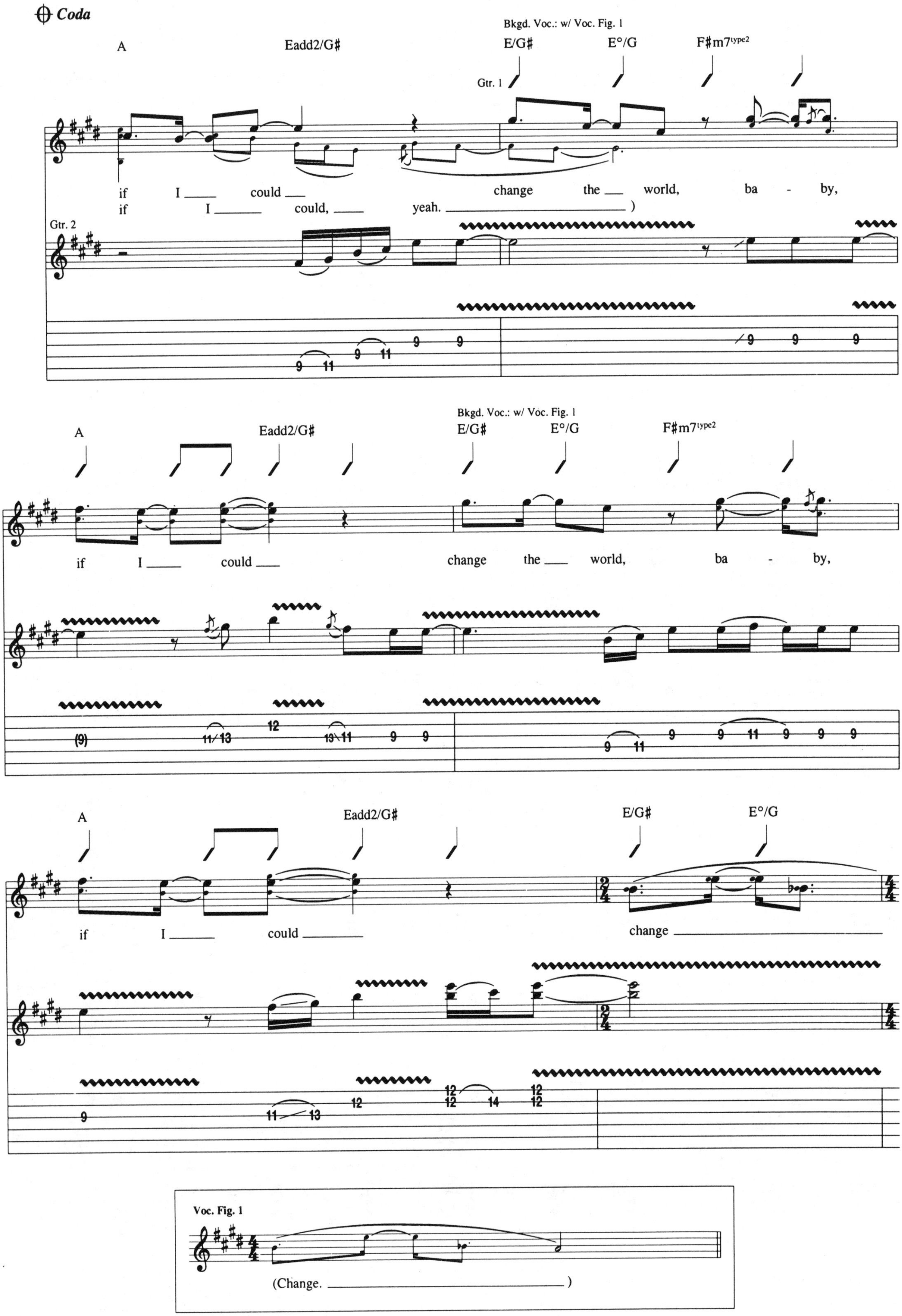
Coda
Bkgd. Voc.: w/ Voc. Fig. 1
A
Eadd2/G#
E/G#
E°/G
F#m7type2
Gtr. 1
if I could change the world, baby,
if I could, yeah.)
Gtr. 2
Bkgd. Voc.: w/ Voc. Fig. 1
A
Eadd2/G#
E/G#
E°/G
F#m7type2
if I could change the world, baby,
A
Eadd2/G#
E/G#
E°/G
if I could change
Voc. Fig. 1
(Change.)

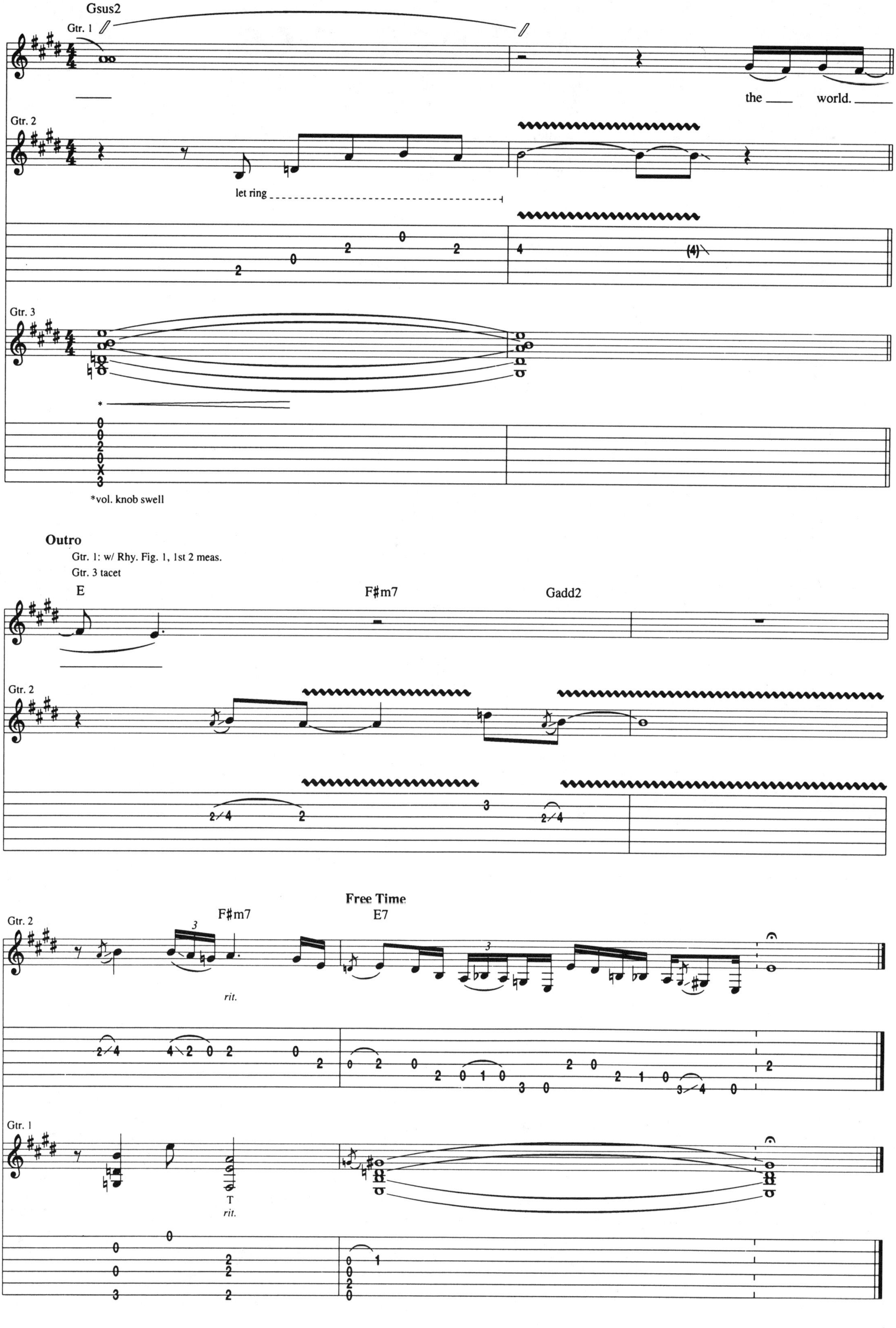
Gsus2
Gtr. 1
the world.
Gtr. 2
let ring
Gtr. 3
*vol. knob swell
Outro
Gtr. 1: w/ Rhy. Fig. 1, 1st 2 meas.
Gtr. 3 tacet
E
F♯m7
Gadd2
Gtr. 2
Gtr. 2
F♯m7
rit.
Free Time
E7
Gtr. 1
rit.

my father's eyes

words & music by eric clapton

Verse
E
A
D/F♯
A/E
E
F♯
B
Emaj7
1. Sail-in' down be -
Gtr. 4
Gtr. 2
Rhy. Fig. 2
End Rhy. Fig. 2
Rhy. Fig. 3
* T
T
Gtr. 3
* T = Thumb on ⑥
Gtr. 3 tacet
Gtr. 4 tacet
F♯
B
C♯/E♯
C♯m/E
F♯
B
Emaj7
hind the sun, wait-in' for the prince to come. Pray - in' for the
Gtr. 4
Gtr. 2

F♯ G♯m C♯/E♯ D/F♯ A/E E
heal - in' rain to re - store my soul a - gain.
Gtr. 2
End Rhy. Fig. 3
Gtr. 3
Pre-Chorus
Gtrs. 2 & 3: w/ Rhy. Figs. 1 & 1A, 2 times, simile
C♯m Amaj7 F♯m B E A
Just a tour - ing, on the run. And how did I get here?
Riff A
Gtr. 4
mp
F♯m B C♯m Amaj7 F♯m B
What have I done? When will all my hopes sur - mise?

Chorus
Gtrs. 2 & 3: w/ Rhy. Figs. 1 & 1A, 1 3/4 times, simile
E A F#m B C#m Amaj7
Voc. Fig. 1
And how will I know him when I look in my fa - ther's eyes?
(Look in - to my fa -
End Riff A Riff A1
F#m B E A F#m B C#m Amaj7
End Voc. Fig. 1
Voc. Fig. 2
My fa-ther's eyes. When I look in my fa - ther's eyes.
- ther's eyes.)
(Look in - to my fa -
F#m B E A D/F# A/E E F#
End Voc. Fig. 2
Gtrs. 2 & 3: w/ Rhy. Fig. 2
My fa-ther's eyes.
- ther's eyes.
End Riff A1
Verse
Gtr. 2: w/ Rhy. Fig. 3
B Emaj7 F# B C#/E# C#m/E F# B
2. Then the light be - gins to shine. I hear those an - cient lul - la - bys.
Gtr. 4
Gtr. 3
Rhy. Fig. 3A

Emaj7 F# G#m C#/E# D/F# A/E E
And _ as I watch _ the seed - ling _ grow, _ feel _ my heart start _ to _ o - ver - flow. _
End Rhy. Fig. 3A
Pre-Chorus
Gtrs. 2 & 3: w/ Rhy. Figs. 1 & 1A, 2 times
C#m Amaj7 F#m B E A F#m B
Where do I find the words to _ say? How do I teach him? What _ do we play? _
Gtr. 4
C#m Amaj7 F#m B E A F#m B
Bit _ by bit, I've _ real - ized _ that's _ when I need them. That's when I need _ my fa -
Chorus
Bkgd. Voc.: w/ Voc. Fig. 1
Gtrs. 2 & 3: w/ Rhy. Figs. 1 & 1A, 1 3/4 times
Gtr. 4: w/ Riff A1
C#m Amaj7 F#m B E A F#m B
- ther's eyes. _ My fa - ther's eyes. ____ That's _ when I need my _ fa -

* Played behind the beat.

E A F#m B C#m Amaj7 F#m B E A F#m A5 E
Gtrs. 2 & 3
Gtr. 4
8va
loco
Gtr. 7
Verse
Gtr. 7 tacet
Gtrs. 2 & 3: w/ Rhy. Figs. 3 & 3A
B Emaj7 F# B C#/E# C#m/E F# B
3. Then the jag - ged edge _ ap - pears _ through the dis - tant clouds _ of tears. _
Emaj7 F# G#m C#/E# D/F# A/E E
I'm _ like a bridge that was washed a - way. _ My _ foun - da - tion's _ one _ made _ of clay. _
mp

Pre-Chorus
Gtrs. 2 & 3: w/ Rhy. Figs. 1 & 1A, 2 times
Gtr. 4: w/ Riff A
C#m Amaj7 F#m B E A F#m B
And as my _ soul _ slides _ down to die, _ how _ could I lose _ him? What did I _ try?
Gtr. 7
C#m Amaj7 F#m B E A F#m B
Bit _ by bit, I've _ real - ized _ that he was here with me and I looked in - to my _ fa -
Outro-Chorus
Bkgd. Voc.: w/ Voc. Fig. 1
Gtrs. 2 & 3: w/ Rhy. Figs. 1 & 1A, till fade
C#m Amaj7 F#m B E A
- ther's eyes. _ My fa - ther's eyes. ______
Gtr. 7
Gtr. 4

Bkgd. Voc.: w/ Voc. Fig. 2
F#m B C#m Amaj7 F#m B
I looked in - to my _ fa - ther's eyes. _
My fa - ther's eyes. _
Riff B
E A F#m B C#m Amaj7
My fa - ther's eyes. ___
(Look in - to my fa -
F#m B E A F#m B
- ther's eyes. _)
My fa - ther's eyes. ___
I looked in - to my _ fa -
End Riff B

Gtr. 4: w/ Riff B, simile, till fade
C#m
Amaj7
F#m
B
E
A
- ther's eyes.
My fa - ther's eyes.
(Look in - to my fa - ther's eyes.)
Gtr. 7
F#m
B
Bkgd. Voc.: w/ Voc. Fig. 1
C#m
Amaj7
F#m
B
Begin Fade
E
A
F#m
B
Bkgd. Voc.: w/ Voc. Fig. 2
C#m
Amaj7
F#m
B
Bkgd. Voc.: w/ Voc. Fig. 3
E
A
F#m
B
let ring
Bkgd. Voc.: w/ Voc. Fig. 1
C#m
Amaj7
F#m
B
E
A
Fade Out

tears in heaven

words & music by eric clapton & will jennings

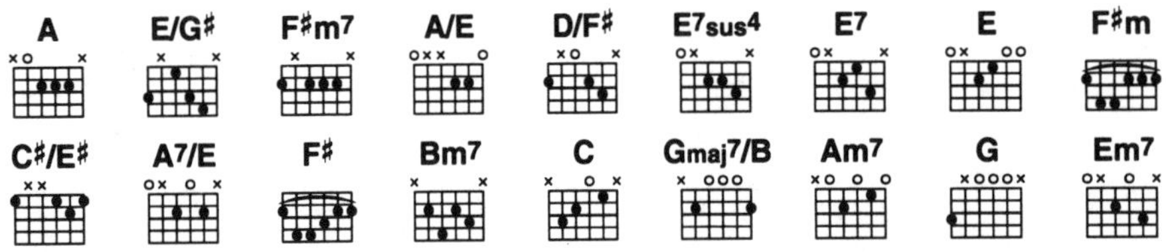

A E/G♯ F♯m7 A/E D/F♯ A/E E
Would it be the same if I saw you in hea - ven?
Would you help me stand if I saw you in hea - ven?
Chorus
F♯m C♯/E♯ A7/E
I must be strong and car - ry on.
I'll find my way through night and day.
F♯ Bm7 E7sus4
'Cause I know I don't be - long here in hea -
'Cause I know I just can't stay here in hea -
To Coda
1.
A E/G♯ F♯m7 A/E D/F♯ E7sus4 E7 A
- ven.

2.
A
E/G♯
F♯m7
A/E
- ven.
D/F♯
E7sus4
E7
A
Gtr. 2 (acous.)
Gtr. 1: cont. sim.
Bridge
C
Gmaj7/B
Am7
D/F♯
G
D/F♯
Time can bring you down, time can bend your knees.
Gtr. 1 (acous.)
Gtr. 2: tacet
Em7
D/F♯
C
Gmaj7/B
Am7
D/F♯
Time can break the heart, have you beg - ging, 'Please.'

G
D/F♯
E
Beg - ging, 'Please.'
Solo
A
E/G♯
F♯m7
A/E
D/F♯
A/E
E
Fig. 1...
(w/pedal steel gtr.)
...Fig. 1 ends
Gtr. 3 (elec.)
Pre
B
mf
w/clean tone
Gtr. 1: w/Fig. 1
Full
Chorus
F♯m
C♯/E♯
A7/E
F♯
Be - yond the door,
there's peace, I'm sure.
And I know
Gtr. 1 (acous.)
Gtr. 3: tacet

Bm7
E7sus4
A
E/G♯
F♯m
there'll be no more tears in hea - ven.
A/E
D/F♯
E7sus4
E7
A
D.𝄋. al Coda
⊕ Coda
A
E/G♯
F♯m7
A/E
- ven.
rall.
D/F♯
E7sus4
E7
A

layla

words & music by eric clapton & jim gordon

Intro

Moderately slow shuffle ♩.=92

1st Verse
C#m7 G#7 C#m7 C D
1. What _ will you do when you get lone - ly? _____ No __ one wait- ing by your
E E7 F#m B E A
__ side. ____ You've _ been run- nin' _ hid - in' much too long, _
F#m B E A
you know it's just your fool - ish pride. __ Lay - la, ___
Chorus
D5 Dm (C) B♭ C D5 N.C. Dm (C) B♭
___ got me on my knees. Lay - la, _____

C D5 N.C. (C) Dm D5 N.C. D5
beg - gin' darl - in', please. _ Lay - la, _____ darl - in' won't you ease my wor - ried
Dm (C) B♭ C N.C. (A) (C)
mind. ___
2nd and 3rd Verses
C#m7 G#7 C#m7 C D
2. Tried to give you _ con- sol - a - tion, __ your old man had let you
3. Make the best of the sit- u - a - tion, __ before I fin - ally go in-
E E7 F#m B E A
down. __ Like _ a __ fool, I fall in love __ with you.
sane. __ Please _ don't say we'll nev- er find __ a way.
Tom (6)
Tom (6)

F#m
A
E
You turned my whole world up - side down.
Tell me all my love's in vain.
Lay - la,
Chorus
Dm (C) B♭
C Dm N.C. D5 Dm (C) B♭
got me on my knees Lay - la,
C D5 N.C. D5 Dm (C) B♭
beg - gin' dar - lin', please. Lay - la,
To Coda
C D5 N.C. D5
dar - lin', won't you ease my wor - ried
1.
Dm (C) B♭
C N.C.
mind.

2.
Dm (C) B♭
C
D5 Dm Dsus2 D5
mind.
Lay-
Chorus
Dm (C) B♭
C
D5 N.C.
Dm (C) B♭
la;
got me on my knees, lay - la,
C
D5 N.C.
D5 (C) B♭
C
Dm N.C.
beg - gin' dar - lin, please. Lay - la,
dar - lin', won't you ease my wor - ried
Dm (C) B♭
C
D5 N.C.
mind.
1/4

Guitar Solo

D.S. al Coda
(C) B♭ C Dm N.C.
Lay - la
1/4
Coda
Dm (C) B♭ C D Dm (C) B♭
mind. Lay - la,
C Dm N.C. D5 Dm (C) B♭ C D5 N.C.
got me on my knees. Lay - la,
beg - gin' dar - lin", please Lay - la,
D5 Dm (C) B♭ C
ritard poco a poco
dar - lin', won't you ease my wor - ried
Rubato
(Dm)
N.C.
mind.

pretending

words & music by jerry lynn williams

G/E
A
How ma - ny times __ must we fail? _____
Liv - ing in a lost _
gliss
P
E5
__ mem - or - y _____ you just re - called. ________
H
E5
G/E
Work - ing on __ the sound of __ the band, __
try - ing to get ___ the mu - sic
Sat - is - fied __ but lost in __ love, _______
situ - a - tions
I get lost __ in al - i - bis, ________
sad -ness can't _____ pre -
A
right,
two __ go out __ work - ing,
three stay home at _
change,
you're never who you used to
think you are,
how
vail,
every - body knows strong
love _____ can't fail. _
Full

E5
to Coda
A
E
night.
strange.
That's when she said she was pre -
Full
D
A
E
D
ten - ding,
like she knew the plan,
P
Full
H
A
E
D
A
E
that's when I knew she was pre - ten - ding,
pre - ten - ding to un - der - stand.
gliss
D
E5
G/E
Pre - ten - ding.
Pre - ten - ding,

D/E
A
E5
Pre - ten -ding.
Pre - ten -ding.
Full
H
P
1.
2.
Solo
E5
G/E
A
E5
Dal 𝄋 al Coda

Coda
E5
A
E
D
Don't be pre - ten - ding
'bout how you feel, _
A
E
D
A
E
Don't be pre - ten - ding
D
A
E
1. D
your love is real.
Don't be pre -
2.
D
E5
Pre - ten - ding.
Pre -

G/E
D/E
A
ten - ding.
Pre - ten - ding.
Full
1/2
E5
Pre - ten - ding.
Fade out
gliss
G/E
H
D/A
A

bad love

words & music by eric clapton & mick jones

Dm C B♭ Bm7
1. Oh what a feel-ing I
2. And now I see that my
gliss
gliss
Bm7/E E A
get when I'm with you,
life has been so blue,
Bm7 Bm7/E E A
you take my heart in-to ev-ery-thing you do.
with all the heart-aches I had till I met you.
And it
But I'm
B♭ C Am B♭ Gm C
makes me sad for the lone-ly peo-ple, I walked that road for so
glad to say now that's all be-hind me, with you here by my

Dm C Dm B♭ C Am B♭
long. Now I know that I'm one of the luck - y peo - ple,
side. And there's no more mem - o - ries to re - mind me,
Gm C G5 Chorus Dm C
your love is mak - ing me strong. Had e - nough bad
your love will keep me a - live.
Gm Dm C Gm
love, I need some - thing I can be proud of. Had e -
Dm C Gm Dm C B♭
nough bad love, no more bad

love.
Dm
C
Gm
gliss
H
T
A
B
Bb
No Chord.
D

D
C G
D C G D
C G D C G
D C G D
C G D C G
D C G D
Dal 𝄋 al 𝄌
T
A
B

Coda
C
B♭
(I've had e -
gliss
gliss
Chorus
Dm
C
Gm
nough
bad
love,
I need
Dm
C
Gm
Dm
C
some - thing I can ___ be proud of. ________
Had e - nough
bad
Gm
Dm
C
B♭
Repeat Chorus and fade.
love,
no more
bad _______
love. ___________

before you accuse me
(take a look at yourself)

words & music by bo diddley

E
self.
go.
You say I'm
B7
spend-ing my mo-ney on oth-er wo-men,
Mom - ma said, "Son, don't
A
tak-ing mo-ney from some-one else.
call my daugh - ter no more."
Fig. 1…
E
1, 2.
B7
(2.) I
(3.) Be -
let ring…
…Fig. 1 ends
3.
B7
Gtr. 1 (elec.)
Gtr. 2: cont in slashes
Solo
Gtr. 2 (elec.)
E5 E6 E5 E6 E5 A5 A6 A7 A6 E5 E6 E5 E6
cont. sim.
Pre

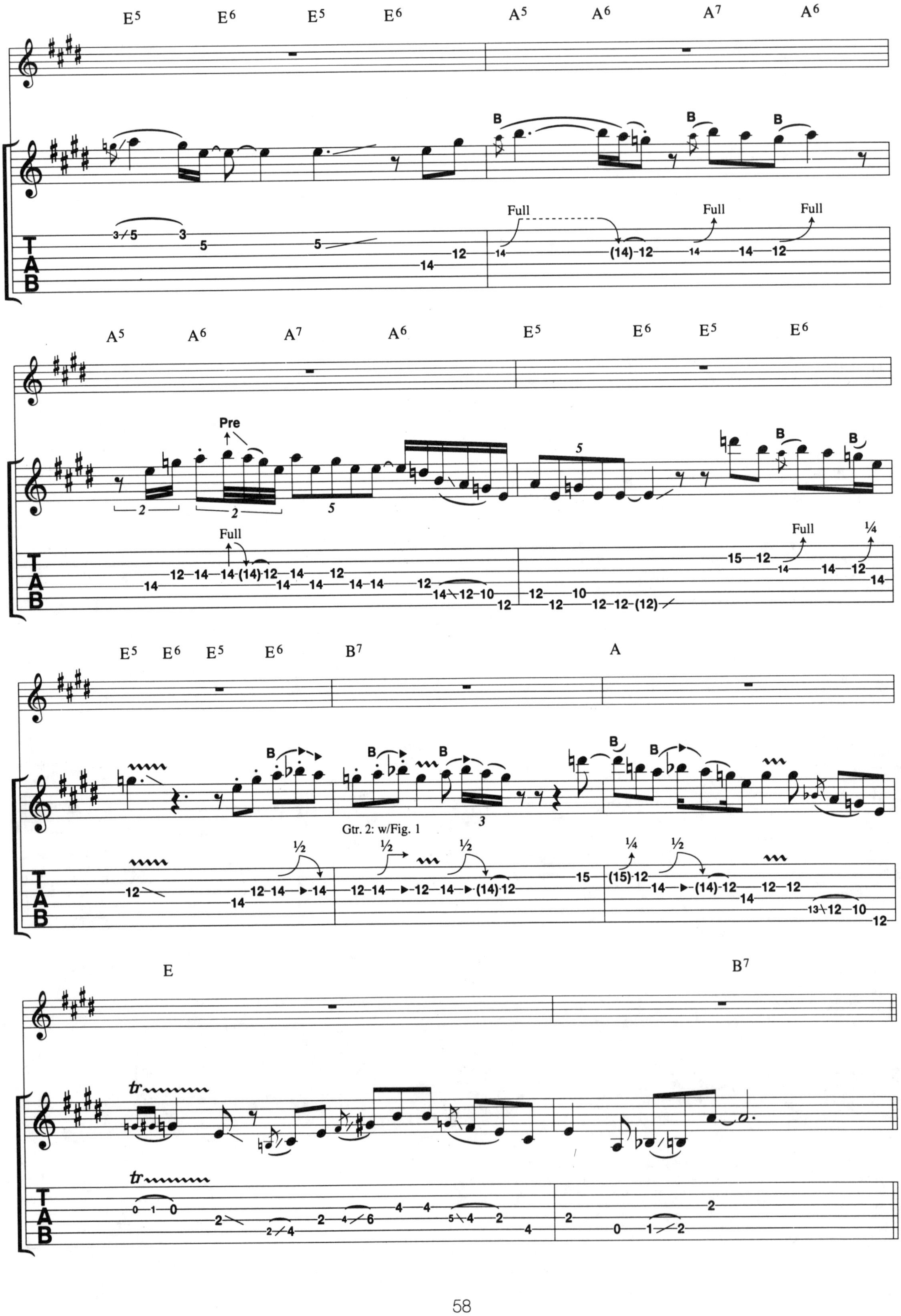
E5 E6 E5 E6 A5 A6 A7 A6
Full
Full
Full
A5 A6 A7 A6 E5 E6 E5 E6
Pre
Full
Full
E5 E6 E5 E6 B7 A
Gtr. 2: w/Fig. 1
E B7

Verse
E
A
E
Come back home_ ba - by, try_ my love_ one more_ time._
Gtr. 2 (elec.)
P.M.
Gtr. 1: doubles ad lib.
A
Come on back_ home ba - by, try_ my love_ one more_
P.M.
E
time._
You know, if I don't_
B7
A
go on and quit_ you, I think I'll lose_ my mind._

E
B7
Gtr. 1: cont. in slashes
Solo
Gtr. 1 (elec.)
E5 E6 E5 E6 E5 A5 A6 A5
cont. sim.
A6 A5 E5 E6 E5 E6 E5
let ring
8va
A5 A6 A5 A6 A5 A6 A5 A6 A5
A6 A5 A6 A5 E5 E6 E5 E6 E5

E5
E6
E5
E6
E5
[B]
(8va)
B
Full
[A]
[E]
B7
loco
5. Be-
Verse
E
A
E
-fore you ac-cuse me,
take a look at your - self
P.M.
let ring...
A
Be - fore you ac-cuse me,
take a look at your -

E
- self.
You say I'm
Full
B7
A
spend - ing my mo - ney on oth - er wo - men,
you're tak - ing mo - ney from some - one
E
B7
else.
Gtr. 1 (elec.)
Gtr. 2: cont. in slashes
Gtr. 1: w/delay
Outro
Gtr. 2 (elec.)
E5 E6 E5 E6 E5 A5 A6 A7 A6 E5 E6 E5 E6
cont. sim.
Full Full
Full
Full
Full
¼

E5 E6 E5 E6 A5 A6 A7 A6
(8va)
A5 A6 A7 A6 E5 E6 E5 E6
(8va)
rake
E5 E6 E5 E6 B7
rake
Gtr. 2: w/Fig. 1
A
[E]
rake
E9
Free time
Gtr. 2 (elec.)

it's in the way that you use it

words & music by eric clapton & robbie robertson

E/G# A C#m B E/G# A C#m B
feel-ings will show.
So don't you ev-er a-buse it,
E/G# A C#m B E/G# A
don't let it go.
(1.) No-bo-dy's right
(2.) I've seen some dark
Verse
C#m B E/G# A C#m B
'til some-bo-dy's wrong, no-bo-dy's weak 'til some-bo-dy's strong.
skies, nev-er like this. Walked on some thin ice, nev-er like this.
E/G# A C#m B E/G# A
No-one gets luck-y 'til luck comes a-long, no-bo-dy's lone-
I've told some white lies, nev-er like this. Looked in-to true

To Coda
C♯m B E/G♯ A
-ly 'til some-bo-dy's wrong.
eyes, nev-er like this.
It's in the way that you use
Chorus
C♯m B E/G♯ A C♯m B
it, it comes and it goes.
E/G♯ A C♯m B E/G♯ A
It's in the way that you use it, well, boy, don't you know.
C♯m B E/G♯ A
Yeah.
Gtr. 2 (elec.)
f w/dist.
Full Full Full Full Full Full Full

Solo
C♯m B E/G♯ A C♯m B
(B) B Full
Full Full Full Full
B B B B B
Full
E/G♯ A C♯m B E/G♯ A
let ring…
B B B B
Full Full Full Full
D.𝄋. al Coda
C♯m B E/G♯ A E/G♯ A
Pre B
Full Full
It's in the way that you use
Gtr. 1 (elec.)
Gtr. 2: tacet
⊕ Coda
F♯/A♯ B D♯m C♯ F♯/A♯ B
It's in the way that you use it,
boy, don't you know.

D♯m C♯ F♯/A♯ B D♯m C♯
So don't you ev - er a - buse it,
Gtr. 2 (elec.)
Gtr. 1 (elec.)
loco
Full
F♯/A♯ B D♯m C♯ F♯/A♯ B
and don't let it go.
Yeah.
Outro
D♯m C♯ F♯/A♯ B D♯mC♯
Pre
F♯/A♯ B D♯m C♯ F♯/A♯ B

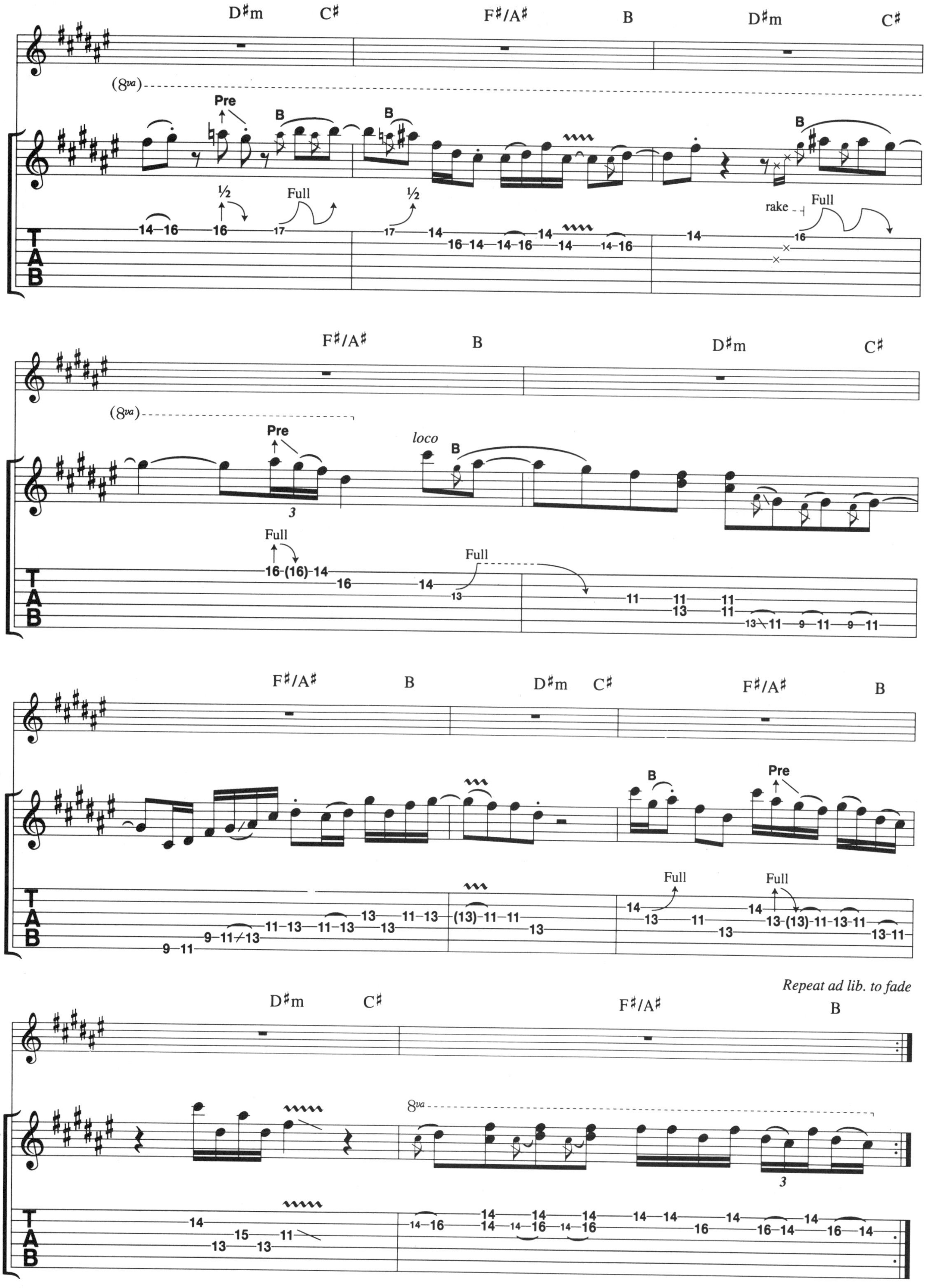
D♯m C♯ F♯/A♯ B D♯m C♯
(8va)
Pre
B
½
Full
rake
T
A
B
F♯/A♯ B D♯m C♯
loco
F♯/A♯ B D♯m C♯ F♯/A♯ B
Repeat ad lib. to fade
D♯m C♯ F♯/A♯ B
8va

forever man

words & music by jerry lynn williams

B♭ C Dm
How man-y times ___ must I ___ tell ___ you, ba - by,
B♭ C Dm
How man-y bridg-es I've __ got to ___ cross? ___
B♭ C Dm Gm
How man-y times __ must __ I ex - plain ___ my - self

B♭
C
Dm
'fore I can talk to the boss,
B♭
C
Dm
'fore I can talk to the boss?
B♭
C
Dm
How man -y times must I say I love you

B♭ C Dm
be - fore you fin - 'ly un - der - stand?
B♭ C Dm Gm B♭ C
Won't you be - my for - ev - er wom - an? I'll try to be your for - ev -
Dm B♭ C Dm
er man, try to be your for - ev - er man.
T
A
B

8va
Guitar Solo
B♭ C Dm B♭ C Dm
Full Full Full Full Full Full 1/4 Full Full
B♭ C Dm Gm B♭ C
Full Full Full Full Full Full Full Full
Dm B♭ C Dm
8va
1/4 Full Full
Guitar II
B♭ C Dm B♭ C
How man-y times must I say I love you be-fore you fin-'ly un-der-
Guitar II: play first verse chord pattern

Dm
Bb
C
Dm
Gm
- stand? __ Won't you be __ my for - ev - er wom - an.
Full
Bb
C
Dm
Bb
C
Try to be __ your for - ev - er ____ man.
Try to be ___ your for - ev - er man. _
Dm
Bb
C
For - ev - er - man, ____ for - ev - er man, __ for - ev - er man. _
Dm
Bb
C
Dm
Gm
For - ev - er man, __ for - ev - er man, _ for - ev - er ______ man.
T
A
B

B♭ C Dm B♭ C
Try to be your for - ev - er man. For - ev - er man, for - ev - er man, for - ev - er
Full Full Full
Dm B♭ C Dm
man. For - ev - er man, for - ev - er man for - ev - er man. For - ev - er man,
8va
Full Full
let ring
B♭ C Dm Gm B♭ C
for - ev - er man, for - ev - er man. Try to be your for - ev - er man.
8va
Full Full
Dm

Guitar Solo
Guitar II: cont. pattern
Full
Full
Full
fade

running on faith

words & music by jerry lynn williams

D G C D
(Rhy. section enters)
(when) love comes o - ver you.
(Gtr. 2)
w/out slide
even gliss
let ring
let ring
let ring
2nd Verse
G D/F♯ Em7 G D
2. Late- ly I('ve) been talk-in' in my sleep.
Can't i-ma-gine what I'd have to say
let ring
Em7 G7 C D
(ex)-'cept my world will be right
(if) love comes back my
1/4
let ring
let ring
Bridge
G C G G7 C
way.
(And) I've al- ways

B(7)
Em
Em7/D
C
G/B
been
one to take each ___ and ev- 'ry day. ________
A7
C
Seems ___ like by now ___ I'd find a love who would care, ______ care just for __
3rd, 4th Verses
* w/Fill 1 (D.S. only)
D
G
D/F#
Em7
me. ___
3.4 Then we'd __ go run-nin' on faith.
* Fills 1 & 2 replace following 3 measures on D.S.
Fill 1
let ring
T
A
B

w/Fill 2 (D.S. only)
To Coda
G D/F♯ Em7 G7 C
All of our dreams will come true, **(and our) world will be right
let ring
let ring
** omit parenthesised lyrics on D.S. only
D G C D D7
love comes o-ver me 'n' you.
even gliss
Guitar Solo
G D/F♯ Em7 C G D/F♯
Em7 G7 C
even gliss
1/4
Fill 2
1/4
T
A
B

D
G
C
let ring
1/4
G
Bridge
C
B7
But ___ I've ___ al- ways been
let ring
Em
Em7/D
C
G/B
A7
one to take each ___ and ev - 'ry day. ___
Seems like ___ by ___
C
D
D.S. al Coda
now ___ I'd find a love who would care, _____ yeah just for me. _______
even gliss
let ring
let ring

Coda
C
D
And our world would be right, ___ love comes ov - er me ___ 'n'
let ring
even gliss.
F6
Cadd9
you, ______ yes it would.
w/out slide
Outro
G Mixolydian
G
F6
Cadd9
Love _ comes _ o - ver _ you. _
Love _ comes oh, ______ o-ver
even gliss.
w/slide
w/out slide
Cadd9
G
F6
Cadd9
you.
Love, ___ love comes o - ver you. __
w/slide
w/out slide

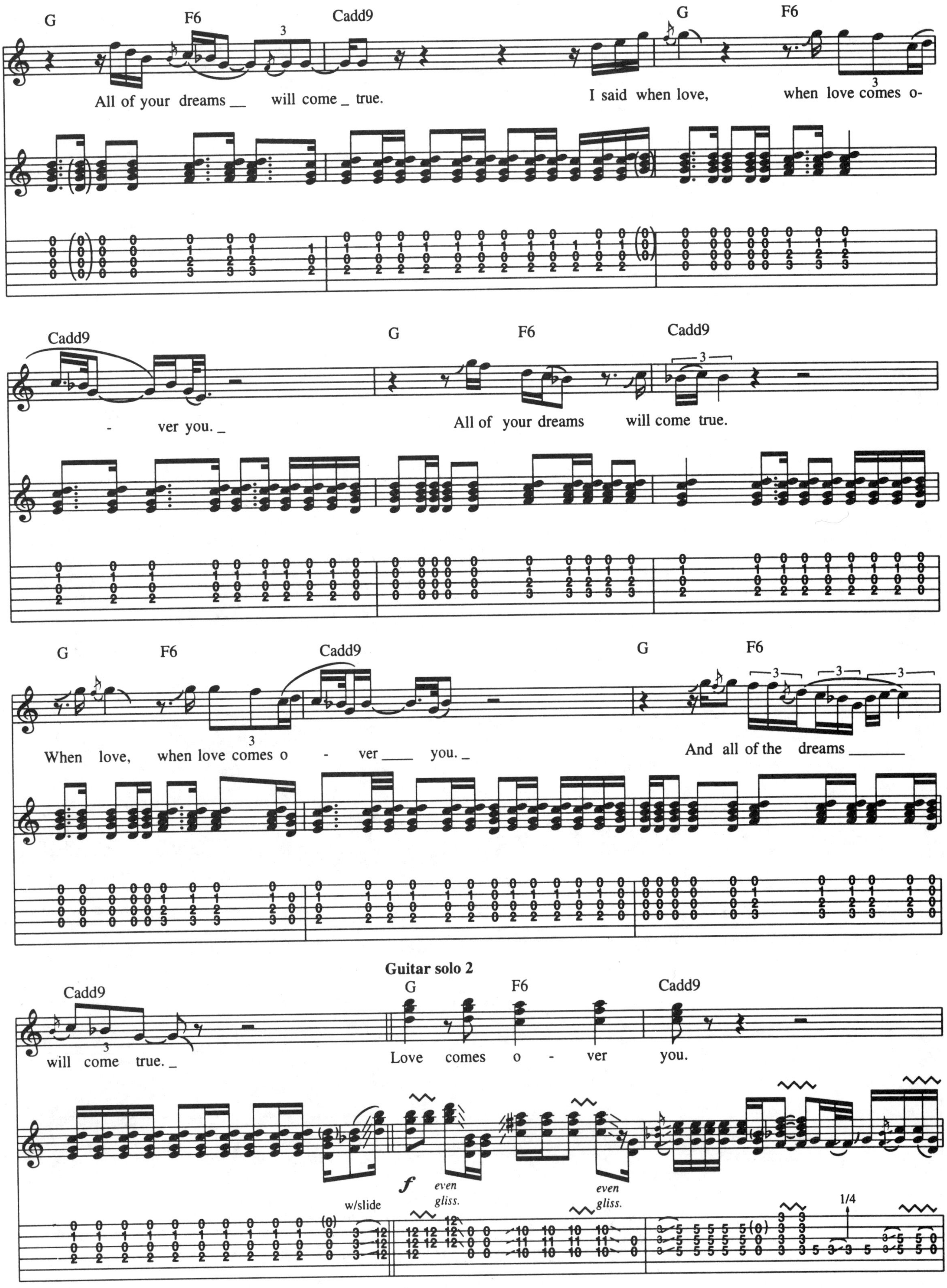

G F6 Cadd9 G F6
All of your dreams _ will come _ true. I said when love, when love comes o-
Cadd9 G F6 Cadd9
- ver you. _ All of your dreams will come true.
G F6 Cadd9 G F6
When love, when love comes o - ver _ you. _ And all of the dreams _
Guitar solo 2
Cadd9 G F6 Cadd9
will come true. _ Love comes o - ver you.
w/slide
even gliss.
even gliss.
1/4

G
F6
Cadd9
Love comes o - ver you.
Yes it does.
1/4
G
F6
Cadd9
Love comes o - ver you.
1/4
G
F6
Cadd9
Love comes o - ver you.
even gliss.
let ring
even gliss.
1/4
G
F6
Cadd9
Love comes o - ver you.
even gliss.
even gliss.
1/4

Love comes o - ver you. Love
let ring
G F6 Cadd9
comes oh, o - ver you.
w/out slide
G F6 Cadd9 G F6
Love comes oh, o - ver you
Love comes o - ver
poco ritard.
ritard.
Rubato
(C)
N.C.
you.
Oo, yeah.
w/slide
1/4
even gliss.

she's waiting

words & music by eric clapton & peter robinson

G C/G Dm/A C/G Dm Am
She's been wait - ing for an -
C G Dm Am C G
oth - er love. Some - one that she can show in - to her heart.
Dm Am C G Dm Am
And when she's fin - 'lly found a strong - - er love, your whole world's gon - na
C G C/G Dm/A C/G
fall a - part. She's wait - ing for an-oth - er love.
G D G C/G Dm/A C/G G D G C/G
She's wait - ing

Dm/A C/G G D G C/G Dm/A C/G
for an-oth - er love.
Dm Am C G Dm Am
You've been a - bus - ing her for far too long.
I see the hun - ger burn - ing in her eyes.
Think you're a king,
An - y fool could see there's
C G B♭ F Csus C
she's your throne.
some-thing wrong.
Get read - y, now, 'cause pret - ty soon
You keep pre - tend - ing not to care,
C/B♭ B♭ F/A F/G C/G B♭ F
to Coda
G C/G
she'll be gone and you'll be on your own.
well, I will hear you sing a diff - rent
Dm/A C/G G D G C/G Dm/A C/G
She's wait - ing
for an-oth - er love.

G D G C/G Dm/A C/G
She's wait -
G D G C/G Dm/A C/G
ing
for an- oth - er love.
G D G C/G Dm/A C/G
Full
G D G C/G Dm/A C/G G D G C/G
Dm/A C/G G D G C/G Dm/A C/G
D. S. 𝄋 al Coda
Full

CODA
tacet (rhythm guitar only)
G C/G Dm/A C/G A D/A
song.
Em/B D/A A D/A Em/B D/A
She's wait-
A E A D/A Em/B D/A A E A D/A
ing for an-oth - er love.
Em/B D/A A E A D/A Em/B D/A
She's wait - ing for an-oth - er love.
A E A D/A Em/B D/A A E A D/A
She's wait - ing.
Em/B D/A A E A D/A Em/B D/A
She's wait - ing. She's wait -
A E A D/A Em/B D/A A E A D/A
ing. She's wait - ing.
(Look-in' for an-oth - er lov - er,
repeat 6 times w/ vocal ad lib.
6 more times a capella
Em/B D/A
She's wait -
hop-in' for a time that she'll find an-oth - er.) Look-in' for an-oth - er lov - er.

river of tears

words & music by eric clapton & simon climie

Dm7
G7sus4
Gtr. 2
Am
D7
Gsus4
Gtr. 1
Riff B
G
F
End Riff B

Verse
Gtr. 2 tacet
Gtr. 1: w/ Riff A, 2 times
C
F
1. It's three miles to the riv - er that would car - ry me a - way,
Dm7
G7sus4
G7
and two miles to the dust - y street that I saw you on to - day.
C
F
It's four miles to my lone - ly room where I'm gon-na hide my face,
Dm7
G7sus4
and a - bout half a mile to the down - town bar that I
G7
Pre-Chorus
Gtr. 1: w/ Riff B
Am
ran from in dis-grace.
Lord how long have I got to keep on run - ning?
Gtr. 2
Rhy. Fill 1
End Rhy. Fill 1
Riff C
w/ fingers
D7
Gsus4
Sev-en hours, sev-en days, or sev-en years? All I know is

G
4:3
since you've been gone,
F
feel like I'm drown-ing
in a riv - er.
Drown - ing
in a riv - er
of
tears.
Drown-ing
Chorus
Gtr. 1: w/ Riff A
C
Voc. Fig. 1
(Oo,
End Riff C
F
in a riv - er.
Dm7
Feel like I'm drown-ing,
drown-ing in a riv -
oo.
Oo,

Interlude
Bkgd. Voc.: w/ Voc. Fig. 1
Gtr. 1: w/ Riff A
G7sus4
G7
C
F
- er.
End Voc. Fig. 1
oo, ___
Riff D
Dm7
G7sus4
End Riff D
Verse
Gtr. 2 tacet
Gtr. 1: w/ Riff A, 2 times
C
F
2. In three more days, I'll leave this town and dis -
Dm7
ap-pear with-out a trace. A year from now, may - be set - tle down
G7sus4
G7
C
where no one knows my face. I wish that I could hold ___ you
F
Dm7
one more time ___ to ease the pain. But my time's run out and I
G7sus4
Gtr. 2: w/ Rhy. Fill 1
G7
got to go, ___ got to run a - way a - gain.

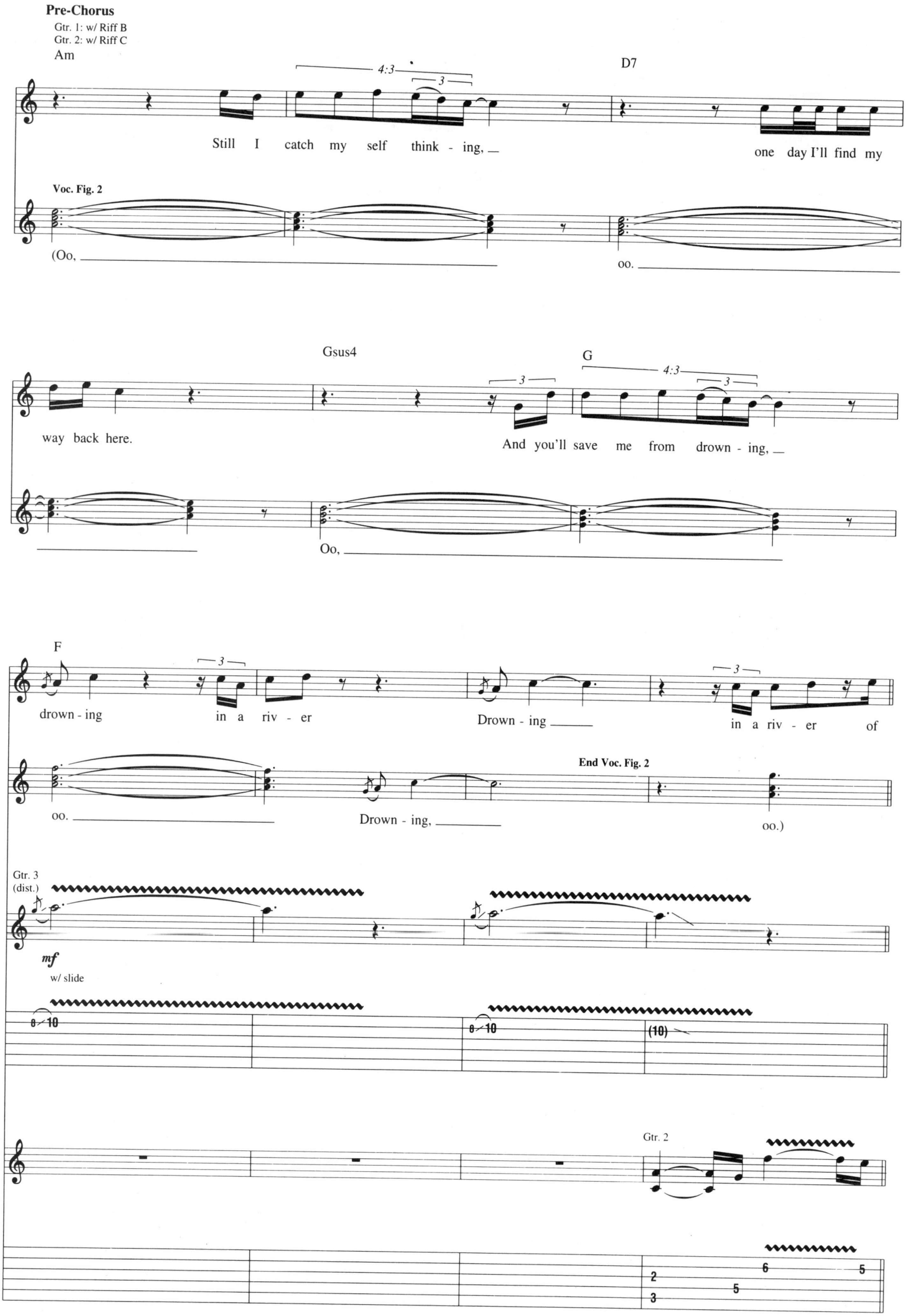
Pre-Chorus
Gtr. 1: w/ Riff B
Gtr. 2: w/ Riff C
Am
D7
Still I catch my self think - ing, one day I'll find my
Voc. Fig. 2
(Oo, oo.
Gsus4
G
way back here. And you'll save me from drown - ing,
Oo,
F
drown - ing in a riv - er Drown - ing in a riv - er of
End Voc. Fig. 2
oo. Drown - ing, oo.)
Gtr. 3 (dist.)
mf
w/ slide
Gtr. 2

Chorus
Bkgd. Voc.: w/ Voc. Fig. 1
Gtr. 1: w/ Riff A
Gtr. 2: w/ Riff D
C
F
tears.
Drown-ing in a riv - er.
Feels like I'm
Gtr. 3
Dm7
G7sus4
G7
drown - ing,
drown - ing in a riv - er.
Lord, how long must this go on?
Gtr. 3
Gtr. 2
Outro
Bkgd. Voc.: w/ Voc. Fig. 1
Gtr. 1: w/ Riff A
Gtr. 2: w/ Riff D, simile
C
F
Dm7
G7sus4
Gtr. 3

Bkgd. Voc.: w/ Voc. Fig. 2
Gtr. 1: w/ Riff B
Gtr. 2: w/ Riff C, simile
Gtr. 2: w/ Rhy. Fill 2
G7
Am
D7
Gsus4
G
F
Gtr. 3 tacet
C
Drown-ing in a riv-er, drown-ing in a riv-er of tears.
(Drown-ing in a riv-er. Drown-ing, oo, oo.)
Gtr. 3
Gtr. 1
Gtr. 2
Rhy. Fill 2
Gtr. 2
T
A
B

(I) get lost

words & music by eric clapton

Verse
Dmaj7/F♯
E13
Bm7
(1.) I'm sor - ry,
(2.) You're an - gry,
(3.) I'm sor - ry,
why should I
why should-n't
why can't I
Gtr. 1 (acous.)
Fig. 1...
Gtr. 2: tacet
Esus4
E
Dmaj7/F♯
E13
say I'm sor - ry?
you be an - gry?
say I'm sor - ry?
If I hurt you,
With what we've been through,
If I hurt you,
...Fig. 1 ends
Bm7
Esus4
E
you know you've hurt me too.
well, I get an - gry too.
you know it hurts me too.
But you
Chorus
Am
Fmaj9
D7/F♯
get lost in - side your tears,
and there is

Gsus4 Esus4 E Am Fmaj9
noth - ing I can do. Cause I get lost in - side my fear,
D7/F♯ To Coda Gsus4 Esus4 E 1. Am Gsus4 G
then I am noth - ing with - out you.
Dmaj7/F♯ E13 Bmaj7 Esus4 E
Gtr. 2
Gtr. 1: cont. sim.
2. Am Gsus4 G D/F♯ F Esus4 E
you. And I am noth - ing with - out

Bridge
F6/9
E7sus4
E7
you. Why should we have tak - en so long, to be
let ring...
A7
D add11/A
F♯7sus4
F♯7
look - ing in - side of our minds?
F6/9
E7sus4
E7
When ev - 'ry - thing we tried went wrong, are we
A7
D add11/A
A7*
wor - ried 'bout what we might find?

F/A A7* Gsus2
Ooh.
Gtr. 2 (acous.)
Gtr. 1: cont. sim.
Interlude
Dmaj7/F♯ E13 Bm7 Esus4 E
Gtr. 1: w/Fig. 1
Dmaj7/F♯ E13 Bm7 Esus4 E
D.%. al Coda
Coda
Gsus4 Esus4 E Am Fmaj9
noth - ing with - out you. And you get lost in - side your tears,

D7/F♯
G sus4
E sus4
E
Am
and there is noth - ing we can do. 'Cause I get
Fmaj9
D7/F♯
G sus4
E sus4
E
lost in - side my fear, then I am noth - ing with - out
Am
Fmaj9
D7/F♯
you. And I am
Two Gtrs. arr. for one
G sus4
E sus4
E
Am
Fmaj9
noth - ing with - out you.

1.
2.
D7/F♯
Gsus4
Esus4
E
Feel like I'm nothing without you.
Like I am
nothing without
Outro
Dmaj7/F♯
E13
Bm7
you.
Gtr. 2 (acous.)
Gtr. 1: w/Fig. 1
Fade out

wonderful tonight

words & music by eric clapton

Verse
G
D add9/F♯
C
(1.) It's late in the eve - ning, she's won-d'ring what clothes to wear. She'll put on her make - up, and brush - es her long blonde hair.
(2.) We'll go to a par - ty, and ev - 'ry - one turns to see this beau - ti - ful la - dy that's walk - ing a - round with me.
(3.) It's time to go home now, and I've got an ach - ing head. So I'll give her the car keys, and she'll help me to bed.
let ring...
D sus2
Chorus
And then she'll ask me, "Do I look al - right?"
And then she'll ask me, "Do you feel al - right?"
And then I'll tell her, as I turn out the light,
T
A
B

Em7
C
Dsus2
To Coda
And I'll say, "Yes, you look won-der-ful to-night."
And I'll say, "Yes, I feel won-der-ful to-night."
I say, "My darling, you were won-der-ful to-night."
1.
G
D add9/F♯
C
B
Full
Dsus2
2.
G
Am
G/B
And I feel
C
D
G
Bm7
Em7
won-der-ful 'cause I see the love light in your eyes, and the won-

C
D sus2
C
D7
- der of it all is that you just don't re - al-ise how much I love
Solo
G
D add9/F♯
C
you.
B
rake
Full
D sus2
G
8va
B
Full
D add9/F♯
C
D sus2
D.%. al Coda
(8va)
Pre
Full
loco
B
Full

Coda
G
Dadd9/F♯
Em7
C
Oh my dar - ling, you were
Free time
D
won - der - ful to - - - - night.
a tempo
Outro
Cadd9
D
Cadd9
Gtr. 1
Kbd. arr. for Gtr.
Fade out
D
Cadd9
D

guitar tablature explained

RHYTHM SLASHES are written above the stave. Strum chords in the rhythm indicated. Round noteheads indicate single notes.

THE MUSICAL STAVE shows pitches and rhythms and is divided by lines into bars. Pitches are named after the first seven letters of the alphabet.

TABLATURE graphically represents the guitar fingerboard. Each horizontal line represents a string, and each number represents a fret.

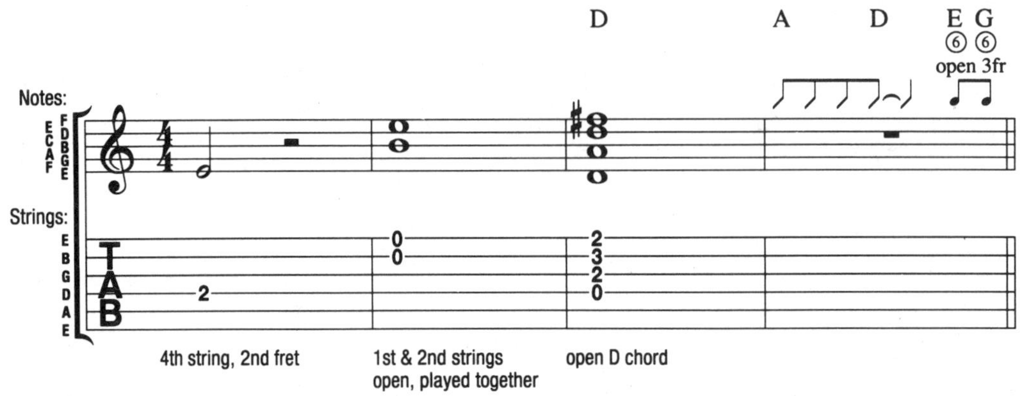

definitions for special guitar notation

SEMI-TONE BEND: Strike the note and bend up a semi-tone (1/2 step).

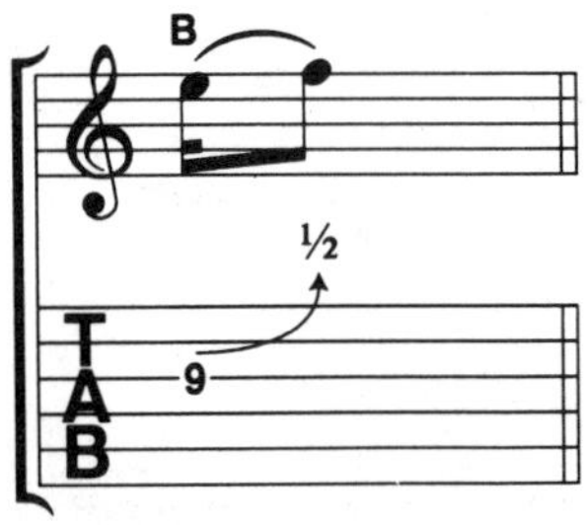

WHOLE-TONE BEND: Strike the note and bend up a whole-tone (whole step).

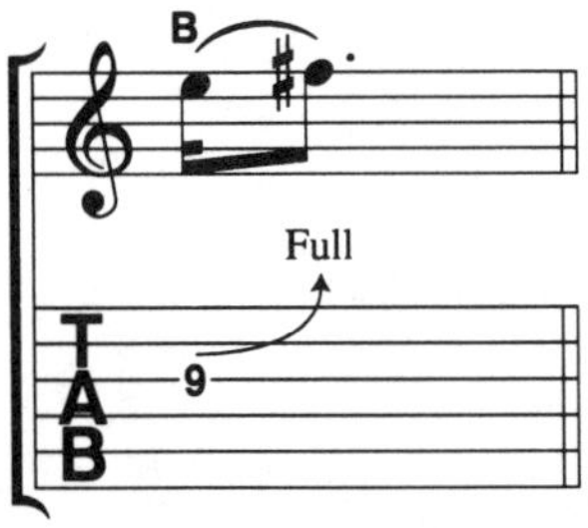

GRACE NOTE BEND: Strike the note and bend as indicated. Play the first note as quickly as possible.

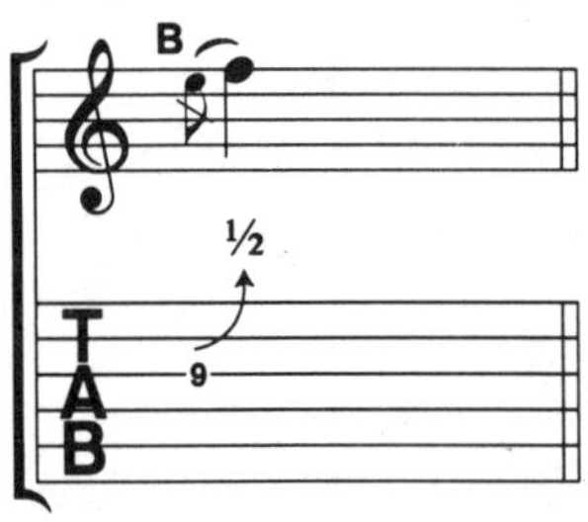

QUARTER-TONE BEND: Strike the note and bend up a 1/4 step.

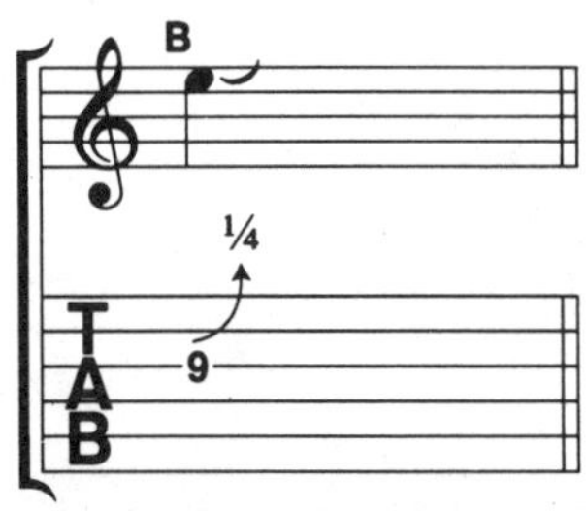

BEND & RELEASE: Strike the note and bend up as indicated, then release back to the original note.

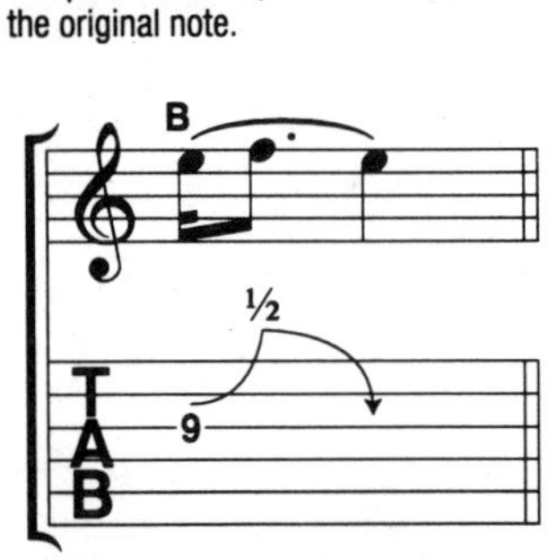

BEND & RESTRIKE: Strike the note and bend as indicated then restrike the string where the symbol occurs.

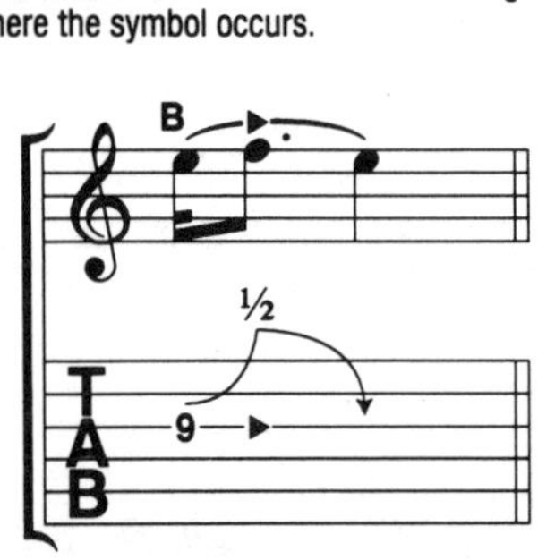

PRE-BEND: Bend the note as indicated, then strike it.

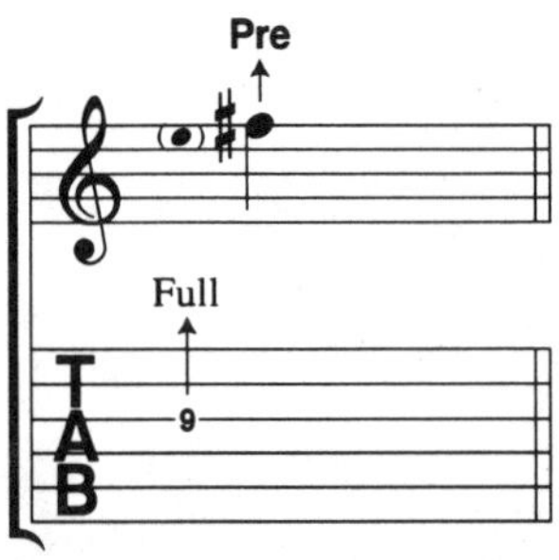

PRE-BEND & RELEASE: Bend the note as indicated. Strike it and release the note back to the original pitch.

HAMMER-ON: Strike the first (lower) note with one finger, then sound the higher note (on the same string) with another finger by fretting it without picking.

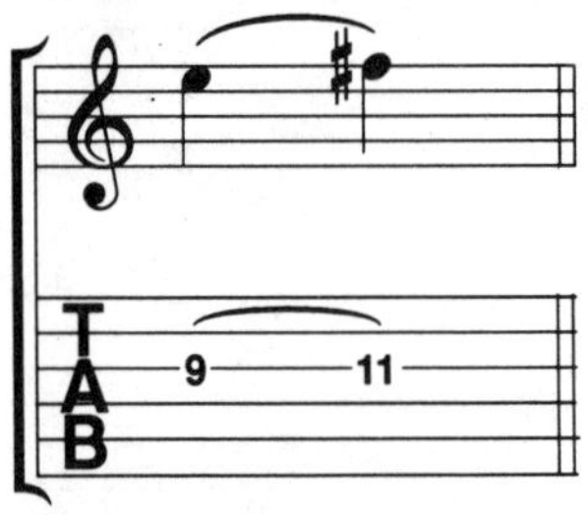

PULL-OFF: Place both fingers on the notes to be sounded. Strike the first note and without picking, pull the finger off to sound the second (lower) note.

LEGATO SLIDE (GLISS): Strike the first note and then slide the same fret-hand finger up or down to the second note. The second note is not struck.

SHIFT SLIDE (GLISS & RESTRIKE): Same as legato slide, except the second note is struck.

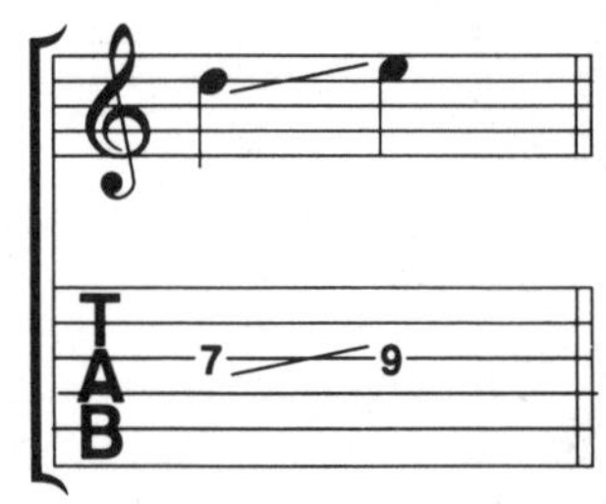

NATURAL HARMONIC: Strike the note while the fret-hand lightly touches the string directly over the fret indicated.

PICK SCRAPE: The edge of the pick is rubbed down (or up) the string, producing a scratchy sound.

PALM MUTING: The note is partially muted by the pick hand lightly touching the string(s) just before the bridge.

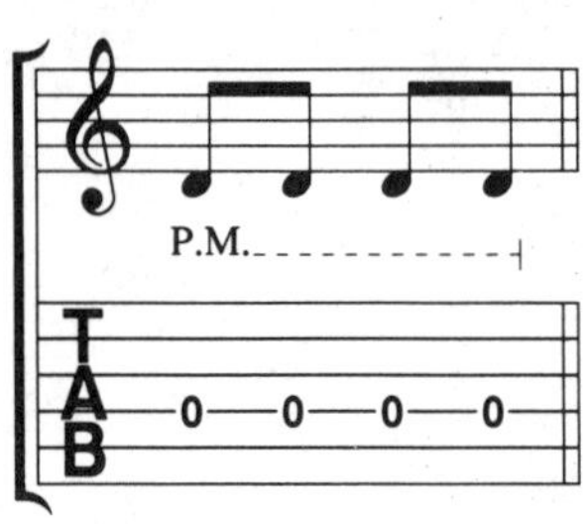

MUFFLED STRINGS: A percussive sound is produced by laying the fret hand across the string(s) without depressing, and striking them with the pick hand.

NOTE: The speed of any bend is indicated by the music notation and tempo.

AM964304 - 2/01 (39413)